Table of Contents

Introduction 5

Part One: God Shows How He Saves

One   *God Preserves Humanity* 9
       Genesis 8:1, Noah

Two   *God Creates a Nation* 19
       Exodus 13:18, The Red Sea

Three   *God Preserves His Nation* 31
       Nehemiah 9:17, Israel the God-Fighter

Part Two: God Provides Salvation for His People

Four   *God Provides a Better Sacrifice* 43
       Psalm 40:6-8, The Incarnation

Five   *God Demonstrates His Love for His People* . . 51
       Romans 5:8, The Cross

Six   *God Raises Jesus from the Dead* 61
       Acts 13:30, The Resurrection

Part Three: God Applies Salvation to His People

Seven   *God Chooses the Foolish and the Weak* . . . 71
       1 Corinthians 1:27, Election

Eight   *God Brings Life Out of Death* 81
       Ephesians 2:4, Salvation

Nine   *God's Firm Foundation Stands* 91
       2 Timothy 2:19, Perseverance

Ten   *Final Thoughts* 99

      Addendum 104
      Endnotes 105
      About Cruciform Press 108

Print ISBN:	978-1-936760-17-6
ePub ISBN:	978-1-936760-19-0
Mobipocket ISBN:	978-1-936760-18-3

CruciformPress.com
email: info@CruciformPress.com
Facebook: http://on.fb.me/Cruciform
Twitter: @CruciformPress
Newsletter: http://bit.ly/CruciformNL

INTRODUCTION

This is a book about two words. Concerning them, the late James Montgomery Boice wrote, "May I put it quite simply? If you understand those two words—'but God'—they will save your soul. If you recall them daily and live by them, they will transform your life completely."

It is no surprise, then, that the human authors of Scripture use this phrase repeatedly to highlight God's grace in every aspect of salvation. From Moses to Paul and just about everywhere in between, "But God" appears time and again at many crucial junctures in Scripture. It is the perfect phrase for highlighting the grace of God against the dark backdrop of human sin.

To the left of "But God" in Scripture appear some of the worst human atrocities, characterized by disobedience and rebellion. To the left of "But God" is hopelessness, darkness, and death. But to its right, following "But God," readers of Scripture will find hope, light, and life. Following God's intervention, the story of Scripture becomes one of grace, righteousness, and justice.

This book has been born out of my desire to better understand these two words, and how they are used in Scripture. Having searched through and referenced every instance of "But God" (or "But he," "But you," etc.), I have found that this phrase is used to describe God's activity in nearly every great salvation story in the Bible.

"But God" marks God's relentless, merciful interventions in human history. It teaches us that God does not wait for us to bring ourselves to him, but that he acts first to bring about our good. It also teaches us of the potential consequences if God were not to act. Scripture shows over and over that without God's intervening grace, without the "But God" statements in the Bible, the world would be completely lost in sin and under judgment.

It may not be a common thing to write a book about two words, but these are no insignificant words. Indeed, everything Dr. Boice wrote above is true. If we understand these two words as the biblical authors use them, we will understand salvation—a salvation that is by grace alone, through Christ alone.

May the reading of this book, and of the biblical "But God" statements it contains, cause you to understand these two words, recall them regularly, and allow them to transform your understanding of God's grace and thus transform your very life.

But / conjunction / (but): 1) Used to introduce something contrasting with what has already been mentioned. 2) Nevertheless; however. 3) On the contrary; in contrast.

God / noun / (How much time do you have?)

Part One
GOD SHOWS HOW HE SAVES

One
GOD PRESERVES HUMANITY

Genesis 8:1, Noah

I had been serving as an associate pastor at a small church in Grand Junction, Colorado, for about a year before I got out and did any real hiking (I'm much more comfortable behind a desk). On the recommendation of a longtime resident, I took a group of at-risk junior high boys to Hanging Lake, a small body of water east of town. Once you reach the trailhead the only way to the lake is on foot; the terrain just gets too rough. So we drove the ninety minutes to the trail, ate lunch, filled our water bottles, and began to climb.

None of us were seasoned hikers, and it didn't take long for our lack of experience to show. While the trail was not spectacularly difficult, we had to work hard, stepping over rocks and traversing small streambeds. The boys probably wished they could have spent the day playing video games.

But then we reached the top and looked out over Hanging Lake. None of us had ever seen anything like it. The water was perfectly clear, with fish darting back and forth in full view. One waterfall fed the lake, and a second one at the opposite side emptied it. We walked along a boardwalk built on the rocky shoreline, the beauty of God's creation mingling with man's ingenuity. And we crossed part of the lake on a fallen tree, careful not to fall into water that was surely as cold as it was clear.

Eventually, we made our way back down the trail (a much easier trip), climbed back into the car, and drove home. I dropped the boys off at their houses, then went home myself.

Thus, the day ended not with a bang but with a bit of a fizzle. We had spent the bulk of our time traveling—in car and on foot. The company had been good and the exercise much needed. Still, we never would have done it if not for the promise of that experience we had in the middle of the day—seeing the lake and enjoying God's creation together. The best part of the day was not the beginning or the end, but the middle.

Saving the Best for the Middle

So often in our great stories and life experiences, the best is saved for last. From the game-winning home run in the bottom of the ninth inning to the dramatic scene just before the credits roll to the encore performance at a great concert, we just seem to love the grand finale. However, many of the stories in the Bible *do not* save the best for last. Like my hiking trip to Hanging Lake, we must look to the middle of many biblical stories to find the best parts, the most meaningful parts.

Take for example the first great salvation story in Scripture—the account of Noah. Reading the flood account is like following a trail across a great mountain: it ascends until it gets to the main point, then descends again. The whole journey is important, but the most glorious part happens at the mountaintop in the middle.

The main points of the biblical story of Noah and the flood, as told in Genesis, appear as follows:[1]

- The earth became incredibly corrupt, to the point where God regretted creating mankind and decided to destroy all human beings (6:1–6:7).
- God chose to save one man (Noah) and gave him instructions for building a large ark in which to survive the flood God would send to destroy the world (6:8–7:25).
- Noah went into the ark, along with his family and some of each kind of animal, and the flood came upon the earth, wiping out all men and beasts outside the ark (7:6–24).

- The flood subsided and Noah left the ark with his family (8:1–19).
- Noah sacrificed to God, God promised never to destroy every living creature again, and God made a covenant with Noah (8:20–9:17)
- Noah planted vineyards in the new world, became drunk from the wine, was mistreated by his son Ham, and died (9:18–29).

At the center point of the flood account, we read:

> ***But God*** remembered Noah and all the beasts and all the livestock that were with him in the ark. And God made a wind blow over the earth, and the waters subsided. (Genesis 8:1)

This verse reveals the main point of the story. Mankind deserved destruction, and even Noah found himself in dire straits, floating with his family and a host of animals in a glorified box over the flood-covered world. At this point, the very heart of the story, we encounter the incredibly important words, "But God." God *remembered* Noah and saved him. God chose not to let humanity die out, instead initiating a salvation plan.

Numbers Show the Center

Shouldn't we perhaps view the exit from the ark as

more important? How about the moment when God makes his covenant with Noah? What about the other portions of the story? How do we know Genesis 8:1 is truly the significant center?

We know by looking to the biblical text itself. The author of Genesis, Moses, wants us to see that everything in the flood account points to God's salvation—the "But God" of 8:1. One way he does this is by emphasizing the divine chronology.

Moses tells the flood story in Genesis 7 and 8 using a numerical/chronological structure, framing the center of the story (Genesis 8:1). Consider these verses:

- And after **seven days** the waters of the flood came upon the earth (7:10).
- The flood continued **forty days** on the earth (7:17a).
- And the waters prevailed on the earth **150 days** (7:24).
- At the end of **150 days** the waters had abated (8:3b).
- At the end of **forty days** Noah opened the window of the ark that he had made and sent forth a raven (8:6–7a).
- He waited another **seven days**, and again he sent forth the dove out of the ark (8:10).

The structure of this text reveals itself clearly. The numbers ascend, from seven to forty to 150, and then descend, from 150 to forty to seven. This is a well-known ancient literary structure called a chiasm, intended to direct the reader's attention toward what occurs in the middle of the story. In this case, the very peak of this biblical mountain is Genesis 8:1–2.

"But God" is at the heart of the flood account.

Grace and Remembering

Perhaps no Bible story suffers from more trivialized telling and retelling than that of the flood. Children's books, toys, and Sunday school curricula often depict Noah in a proportionally tiny ark sailing along happily with a few cheerful animals. Such presentations typically focus on either the animals or Noah's piety.

But the biblical story of Noah is no mere morality tale. The point is not that the rest of the world was really bad but Noah was really good, so God decided to save him. In fact, Noah does not even serve as the main character in the story. The main player in the biblical flood account is God. The entire story points to *him*.

We have already seen how the chiasm of this story centers the account on 8:1, "But God remembered Noah" But we also need to understand that when the Bible speaks of God "remembering" someone, it does not mean he had previously forgotten about that person. It means he is choosing to work *on the person's behalf*, and *for his good*.[2] Certainly, this describes what happens in the flood account. With the rest of the world lying dead under a sea of judgment and Noah floating aimlessly above with a slew of animals, God *remembered* him; he would not let Noah die. God saved him by reversing the flood and giving Noah a new world in which to live.

In other words, the flood story is about God's grace. Even the first significant statement made about Noah tells us more about God's grace than about Noah himself: "So the LORD said, 'I will blot out man whom I have created from the face of the land, man and animals and creeping things and birds of the heavens, for I am sorry that I have made them.' *But Noah found favor in the eyes of the LORD*" (Genesis 6:7–8). The word "favor" might not seem especially meaningful to us, but the Hebrew word translated here as "favor" can also be translated as "grace." In fact, the King James Version translators used that very word, "But Noah found *grace* in the eyes of the LORD."

This is the first time we find the word *grace* in Scripture.

Amid a sin-corrupted world, God looked at Noah and decided to treat him differently. He decided not to give him the judgment that his sins deserved, but instead to bless him and to preserve the entire human race through him. Only *after* noting that Noah received grace did Moses recount Noah's righteousness (Genesis 6:9). This order conveys something significant. Henry Morris writes:

> Note the consistent biblical order here. First, Noah "found grace." Then Noah was "a just man" (that is, "justified" or "declared to be righteous"). Thus, he was "perfect in his generations" (or "complete," in so far as God's records are concerned), and therefore he was able to "walk with God." Salvation in any era is exactly in this way. By sovereign grace, received through faith, the believer is justified before God and declared to be complete in him. Only as a result of, and on the basis of, this glorious gift of grace, can one then "walk" in fellowship with God, showing the genuineness of his faith by his works.[3]

The biblical account of the flood does not exist to glorify Noah or to tell a cute story about animals but to exalt the Lord as the God who saves. God saves men by his grace, through the cross, and he saves them unto good deeds and obedience. Noah was a righteous man only because he received the grace of God. He was a sinner[4] who needed God to remember him if he would survive the judgment God had sent upon the earth. And God did so.

The flood account takes us up the mountain of God's grace and back down, centering on this one glorious point: the world was doomed to destruction, *but God* chose to remember one man and show him grace. This narrative sets the tone for every great salvation story in the Bible—God saves people by his own doing, keeping them from the judgment they rightfully deserve. "But God," as we will continue to see, plays an absolutely necessary role in every great salvation epic in Scripture.

But God remembered Noah and all the beasts and all the livestock that were with him in the ark. And God made a wind blow over the earth, and the waters subsided.

Next:

The "But God" moment when God began to form his people into a nation.

Two
GOD CREATES A NATION

Exodus 13:18, The Red Sea

As the story line of Scripture progresses, the scope of God's salvation plan expands, taking on a corporate aspect. Beginning with Abraham, God repeatedly says, "I will make of you a great nation" (Genesis 12:2). The remainder of the book of Genesis shows how God began to form this nation, increasing its size and molding its collective character.

The process starts with Abraham and continues in the families of his son Isaac and his grandson Jacob. God changes Jacob's name to Israel (Genesis 32), thereby renaming a nation that would grow rather rapidly, due to his eventual twelve sons. When we come to the book of Exodus, we find that the nation of Israel has grown exceedingly large (Exodus 1:7), yet Egypt, the world superpower of the day, has enslaved them. These Israelites are a pitiable, oppressed people, with no way out of their predicament. In order for them to become the great nation that God had promised they would be, something extraordinary must happen. They need a "But God" event.

The Transformation Begins

The transformation of Israel begins when God sends Moses to deliver the people from bondage. Through Moses, God works wonder after wonder to bring about the Israelites' deliverance, yet Pharaoh repeatedly refuses to let them go. Only after God brings about the death of all Egyptian firstborns (sparing the Israelites through the Passover sacrifice) does Pharaoh free Israel from bondage.

So a couple of million souls, from infants to the elderly—a people who have known nothing but slavery, poverty, and bondage for hundreds of years—march out into the desert. What next? Which way do they go?

Neither Moses nor the Israelites had to answer those questions. The God who had done wonders on their behalf had not finished doing them good and leading them. The Israelites did not need to determine their own route out of Egypt. Instead, God led them with a cloud by day and a pillar of fire by night (Exodus 13:21).

And he led them on an unexpected route—not the easiest or most direct route to the Promised Land.

Not even close. But God had good reasons for this. One reason was that he did not want them to meet war too soon. Exodus 13:17 says, "When Pharaoh let the people go, God did not lead them by way of the land of the Philistines, although that was near. For God said, 'Lest the people change their minds when they see war and return to Egypt.'" God dealt graciously with the Israelites, who had never known battle. Some Bible scholars believe that they were not even armed with real weapons at this point.[5] In any event, they were certainly not ready to fight, and God kindly protected them from needing to fight too soon.

But God had a second reason for leading the Israelites to the Red Sea—so that he could fight for them.

After releasing the Israelites to the desert where they followed the pillar and the cloud, Pharaoh changed his mind and came after them in order to enslave them again. An enslaved Israel could never become the nation God had promised they would be, and Israel could not match the strength of Pharaoh's soldiers and chariots, so God had to act. And Scripture reveals that the sovereign, omniscient God had *already* acted. Before Pharaoh had his latest (and last) change of heart, the necessary "But God" moment had already taken place:

> *But God* led the people around by the way of the wilderness toward the Red Sea. (Exodus 13:18a).

Pharaoh thought he had set the stage for a dramatic moment of victory. But kings do not set such stages; God does. God had indeed set this stage for a dramatic moment. It would not, however, be a moment of victory for Pharaoh.

Dry Land, Wet Walls

At first glance, it seems that the Israelites were in a horrid predicament, backed up against the sea with nowhere for retreat. If they had any sense that the Egyptians might come after them (and they should have, given how fickle Pharaoh had been), this was not a smart place to go. But according to the biblical account, God *led* them there. They became backed up against the Red Sea because God wanted them there.

Israel's crossing of the Red Sea has been immortalized not only in the biblical record, but also in Cecil B. DeMille's landmark film, *The Ten Commandments*. The most visually impressive scene in the movie shows the parting of the Red Sea so that the Israelites could walk through on dry land. Operating in the days before computer-generated special effects, DeMille went to great lengths to re-create this event. He refused to use any hand-drawn animation to enhance the scene but creatively filmed large amounts of water in various ways, splicing the shots together to achieve the finished effect. No wonder the film won the 1956 Academy Award for best visual effects.

DeMille rightly put great effort into that scene, for it was central not only to the movie, but also to God's story of salvation. The Red Sea was where God once and for all "saved Israel . . . from the hand of the Egyptians," where "Israel saw the great power that the LORD used against the Egyptians," and where "the people feared the LORD, and . . . believed in the LORD and in his servant Moses" (Exodus 14:30–31). Here we see Israel's formal beginning as a nation—the people's initiation, of sorts, as the people of God. Paul writes that "all [Israel] were baptized into Moses in the cloud and in the sea" (1 Corinthians 10:2). The Red Sea crossing became a truly monumental event in Israel's history.

Israel's deliverance that day was all of God, as he parted the waters so that Israel could walk through on dry land. Meanwhile, he held the Egyptians back so that they could not pursue until all the Israelites had passed through. When God then allowed the Egyptians to follow Israel into the sea, the waters closed upon them so that they were completely defeated. That day, Israel became an independent nation, not owing to any effort of the people, but only to God's deliverance.

In September 2010, a team from the National Center for Atmospheric Research determined that the Red Sea crossing could have been accomplished by a natural phenomenon known as "wind setdown." They demonstrated how, under the right circumstances, a 63-mph wind, blowing for twelve hours, could push a small body of water aside so that people could cross on dry land. Thus, they concluded that the Red Sea crossing could have been achieved by entirely natural circumstances.[6]

However, the phenomenon the researchers described does not come close to what we read in Scripture. In Exodus, "the people of Israel went into the midst of the sea on dry ground, the waters being a wall to them on their right hand and on their left" (Exodus 14:22). We read also that when God closed the sea, "The waters returned and covered the chariots and the horsemen; of all the host of Pharaoh that had followed them into the sea, not one of them remained" (Exodus 14:28).

This was not a mere streambed pushed aside by a heavy wind. This body of water was large enough to submerge an entire army—and God parted it, held it back, and then released it with perfect timing. God delivered Israel in such a way that no Israelite could attribute it to anything other than the Lord's great power and strength. Miriam's spontaneous, infectious celebration (Exodus 15:20-21) then symbolized a new courage and joy that God had planted in the hearts of his people. The transformation of that people, from oppressed slaves to great nation, had begun. They started to see their God as both powerful and faithful, and they began to understand that he had indeed called them as his own. Ever since that day, God's chosen ones have celebrated that deliverance and the process of transformation it initiated.

A Newborn, Abandoned

Why did God choose to defend and embrace this particular people at this particular time? Not because they were impressive, or powerful, or wealthy, or well-organized, or especially promising in any way. It would be an understatement to say that this people had failed to distinguish themselves; without ever having been invaded or conquered, they had become a nation of slaves living within and serving a nation of non-slaves. Later in Scripture, God remembers Israel's degree of helplessness when he called them as his chosen people. In vivid language, he tells them there was nothing in them that was of value to him:

> And as for your birth, on the day you were born your cord was not cut, nor were you washed with water to cleanse you, nor rubbed with salt, nor wrapped in swaddling cloths. No eye

pitied you, to do any of these things to you out of compassion for you, but you were cast out on the open field, for you were abhorred, on the day that you were born. And when I passed by you and saw you wallowing in your blood, I said to you in your blood, "Live!" I said to you in your blood, "Live!" (Ezekiel 16:4–6)

The picture God paints of Israel in its beginning is not that of a powerful nation but of an abandoned orphan, a helpless baby entirely dependent on others for life. Yet God adopted the people and turned them into a nation unique in all the earth—a nation created not by military strength or political strategy, but by God himself.

God Delights to Help the Helpless

One of my collegiate textbooks on world history consisted of a collection of surveys about great ancient nations. It covered Egypt, Greece, Rome, and others, including Israel. The authors wrote that Israel had done nothing significant to benefit the world in the areas of art, music, literature, military prowess, or political innovation. Nevertheless, the authors claimed that Israel had to be ranked among the great nations of history because of its marvelous religious ingenuity. It was a mystery to the authors how this small nation, completely insignificant from a historical perspective, could have concocted a religion so magnificent that it has influenced nearly every facet of world history since then.

Only the Bible solves this mystery. The biblical story shows that "religious innovation" does not account for Israel's significance. Only the marvelous grace of God does. The Israelites had surely done nothing to commend themselves to God or man:

- Prior to their initiation as a nation in the crossing of the Red Sea, Israel had been a band of slaves in Egypt.
- Prior to their slavery in Egypt, they had been an insignificant family marked by petty jealousy and infighting.
- Prior to that, their namesake, Israel (Jacob), had been known primarily as a deceiver.
- Prior to that, Abraham had been an old man with a barren wife.

At no single point in the history of Israel do the Israelites as a people appear strong or powerful. But God delights in helping the weak. And he delights in choosing those who have no ability to save themselves.

Later in Israel's history, when God gave his people his law, he commanded them to bring tithes to the temple once a year. When they brought their offerings, they recited the following words:

> A wandering Aramean was my father. And he went down into Egypt and sojourned there, few in number, and there he became a nation, great, mighty, and populous. And the Egyptians treated us harshly and humiliated us and laid on us hard labor. Then we cried to the LORD, the God of our fathers, and the LORD heard our voice and saw our affliction, our toil, and our oppression. And the LORD brought us out of Egypt with a mighty hand and an outstretched arm, with great deeds of terror, with signs and wonders. (Deuteronomy 26:5–8)

If this story did not reference God, it would seem ridiculous. Tribes of nomadic shepherds do not grow into a nation of poor, oppressed slaves and then simply decide to walk out on their slave masters. But God's work on Israel's behalf causes this story to make sense.

God did not choose some powerful nation to advance his plan of salvation. He chose slaves instead of masters, and he did all the work for them. He showed them that he is the one true God, and that he had made them a nation by his might, not their own. He backed them into an inescapable corner, with the sea behind them and the world's most powerful army advancing toward them. He alone delivered them from this predicament, establishing them as a nation.

He graciously orchestrated every step along the way so that these things could not be any more apparent to his people. In this way, he forever changed how the people thought about him and about themselves in relation to him. The transformation had begun.

But God led the people around by the way of the wilderness toward the Red Sea.

Next:

A "But God" statement that assures even rebels of God's unfailing love.

Three
GOD PRESERVES HIS NATION

Nehemiah 9:17, Israel the God-Fighter

Long before any Israelites went to Egypt, the patriarch Jacob did some wandering of his own: after many years away from home, he found himself wandering back. But he feared running into his twin brother Esau, whom he had defrauded out of their father's blessing, so he formulated a plan to counteract what he imagined as Esau's impending attack. Part of the plan involved sending the rest of his traveling party away. But something happened that Jacob did not expect: "Jacob was left alone. And a man wrestled with him until the breaking of the day" (Genesis 32:24).

Jacob undoubtedly thought this man was Esau himself or one of his representatives, so he fought vigorously. The struggle reached a breaking point when the man touched Jacob's hip and popped it out of its socket, but even then Jacob would not give up. When the man asked Jacob to let him go, Jacob (probably realizing at this point that his opponent was no mere man) refused to do so unless the man blessed him.

His opponent, of course, was not a man but God (Genesis 32:30). When Jacob asked God to bless him, God said, "Your name shall no longer be called Jacob, but Israel, for you have striven with God and with men, and have prevailed" (Genesis 32:28). The name *Israel* meant "God fighter," or one who struggles with God. It seemed fitting that this name would transfer to God's chosen nation, for the Israelites' story in the Old Testament features constant battle against their Lord.

Human Failure, Divine Faithfulness

Following their deliverance from Egypt, the Israelites suffered one failure after another, much of it rooted in ingratitude toward God. They complained about a lack of water (Exodus 15:24) and put God to the test about it (Exodus 17:2–3). They complained about the food God miraculously gave them (Numbers 11:6). They did not obey the Sabbath instructions God gave them (Exodus 16:27–28). In their most famous act of rebellion, they fashioned a golden calf to serve as an object of worship (Exodus 32).

The Israelites' struggle with God continued even after they reached the Promised Land. The book of Judges recounts how Israel the God-Fighter committed one act of defiance after another, each rebellion bringing divine discipline in the form of oppression by another nation. Later, the Israelites insisted that God give them a king when *they* wanted one, not when he had intended, so God gave them the wicked King Saul. After later prospering, though briefly, under Kings David and Solomon, Israel then split into two kingdoms. Continuing idolatry led the northern kingdom, still known as Israel, to destruction by the Assyrians. The people of the southern kingdom, called Judah, did not learn from this, and some time later the Babylonians carried them into captivity, leaving their capital city, Jerusalem, a heap of rubble.

But through all these failures and catastrophes, God never abandoned his people. He kept his promises and remained faithful to them. During the era of the Judges, each time the people were oppressed but then repented, God sent a leader to deliver them. Likewise, when the people of Judah were exiled in Babylon, God eventually brought them back.

This return to the homeland is documented in the books of Ezra and Nehemiah. At one point, Nehemiah recorded a magnificent prayer that recounted the grace of God throughout the long history of Israel (Nehemiah 9). Tracing the story from the Exodus out of Egypt up until the time of the prophets, he showed how God's people had continually rebelled, but God had been continually gracious. The contrast is stark, and it highlights the fact that God shows grace even to proud rebels.

In this prayer, Nehemiah records the following statement concerning a specific point in the history of his Israelite forefathers more than 700 years earlier:

> They refused to obey and were not mindful of the wonders that you performed among them, but they stiffened their neck and appointed a leader to return to their slavery in Egypt. *But you* are a God ready to forgive, gracious and merciful, slow to anger and abounding in steadfast love, and did not forsake them. (Nehemiah 9:17)

Here we encounter yet another significant "But God" statement.

God Never Abandons His People

Numbers 14 tells the story that is specifically referred to in Nehemiah 9:17. As the people of Israel prepared to cross the Jordan into the Promised Land, they received a report that the inhabitants of Canaan—the land God had promised to give to them—were giant men of great strength. The Israelites panicked. "Would that we had died in the land of Egypt! Or would that we had died in this wilderness!" they said (Numbers 14:2). They openly doubted God's goodness, despite all that he had done for them, stating, "Why is the LORD bringing us into this land, to fall by the sword? Our wives and little ones will become a prey" (Numbers 14:3a). Their doubt led them to hatch a new plan: "'Would it not be better for us to go back to Egypt?' And they said to one another, 'Let us choose a leader and go back to Egypt'" (Numbers 14:3b–4).

Consider what the Israelites do here:

- Even though God had spared every firstborn Israelite child from the Passover plague, the people doubted that he could save their children from the inhabitants of Canaan.
- Even though he had destroyed the most powerful army on Earth for their sake, they doubted he could or would protect them from less powerful people groups.
- Even though he had always worked for their good, they had come to believe he was working *against them*.

This portion of the prayer in Nehemiah referred to one particular generation of the Israelite people, but these words could apply to the nation of Israel at any point throughout the Old Testament. As a people, Israel the God-fighter was obstinate, disobedient, and idolatrous, but God was faithful, forgiving, and loving. They constantly abandoned God even though he did only good to them, and he never abandoned them although they constantly behaved wickedly toward him. In spite of all this, God continued to love and bless them. He did not break his covenant, though they had given him every possible reason (humanly speaking) to do so.

This is how God works. Even when his people repeatedly, predictably, and egregiously flout his laws and ignore his Word, God may discipline us for a time so that we may learn, but he does not abandon us forever. This God keeps his covenants.

God Keeps His Covenant Forever

Israel's history in the Old Testament was a history of covenant failure. But for every failure, a "But God" moment kept them in place as God's chosen people.

God had made it clear from the beginning that it would be this way—that he, not his people, would be the primary one keeping the covenant. When Abraham requested that God confirm his promise in Genesis 15, God told him to cut several animals in half, and Abraham did so. Then something strange occurred. "When the sun had gone down and it was

36

dark, behold, a smoking fire pot and a flaming torch passed between these pieces. On that day the LORD made a covenant with Abram, saying, 'To your offspring I give this land'" (Genesis 15:17–18a).

This ceremony involving the dividing of animals was an ancient way of ratifying a covenant. Animals were ripped in two and the covenant parties passed between the pieces, signifying that they deserved the same fate as the animals if they violated the terms of the covenant. But Abraham did not pass through the pieces—only God did so. "For when God made a promise to Abraham, since he had no one greater by whom to swear, he swore by himself" (Hebrews 6:13). The responsibility fell on God alone to keep his promise, and God always keeps his promises.

Grace, Forgiveness, Mercy

God keeps his promises because it is in his nature to do so. The great "But God" statement of Nehemiah 9:17 shows that God continued to bless his people not because they earned it, but because of his nature. God is described as "ready to forgive, gracious and merciful, slow to anger and abounding in steadfast love." This is a clear nod to the words God spoke when he passed before Moses on Mount Sinai. Moses asked God, "Please show me your glory." In response, God told Moses, "I will make all my goodness pass before you" (Exodus 33:18–19a).

When Moses asked to see God's *glory*—that is, his essential nature—God promised to show Moses his *goodness*. God's essential nature is *goodness*, which he described as being "merciful and gracious, slow to anger, and abounding in steadfast love and faithfulness" (Exodus 34:6).

God did not abandon his disobedient people because his nature would not allow it. Though he punished them by bringing the consequences of their sin upon them, he did not leave them, because they were his people and he loved them. He expressed this in heart-wrenching words to Hosea: "How can I give you up, O Ephraim? How can I hand you over, O Israel? . . . My heart recoils within me; my compassion grows warm and tender" (Hosea 11:8).

God could not give his people up because to do so would mean removing a part of himself—the part that loves unconditionally in accordance with his promises. Though the God-fighters rebelled against God, doubted his goodness, and repeatedly ignored his messengers, nothing they did could change God's nature.

History, Unvarnished

In London's British Museum sits a large hexagonal cylinder, engraved with ancient writings on each side. Known as the Taylor Prism, it contains the annals of the Assyrian King Sennacherib from the seventh and eighth centuries BC. After recounting many of Sennacherib's conquests, it describes his attack on King Hezekiah and God's people in Jerusalem. The Scriptures tell the story of this attack in 2 Kings 19. According to the Bible, Sennacherib's siege of Jerusalem ended when "the angel of the LORD went out and struck down 185,000 in the camp of the Assyrians" (2 Kings 19:35). The account on the Taylor Prism differs a bit, recounting the siege as a victory, not a defeat, with Sennacherib "shutting up Hezekiah in Jerusalem 'like a caged bird'"[7] and then leaving when Hezekiah provided a tribute payment. This is interesting and odd, because Sennacherib's boasts usually recounted his complete destruction of cities and the death of their kings. That's how Sennacherib liked to do it. Why not rather take that same approach with a city that seemed helpless before him? Why would he call it a great victory to be bought off by Hezekiah and then leave peacefully?

Simple—the Assyrians did not dare record a defeat like the one described in Scripture: to do so would have affronted not only their king, but also their gods. Indeed, most ancient nations did not record their defeats and shameful acts for this very reason.

This explains the discrepancy between the biblical account and the one that appears on the

Taylor Prism. Moreover, it reveals the oddness of Scripture: Israel did not record its history like other nations recorded theirs. The Old Testament tells not only of Israel's victories and righteous acts, but also of its defeats and sins. Nobody is spared, not even the most highly regarded Israelites. Moses cannot enter the Promised Land because of his sinful pride. David receives severe punishment for his adulterous affair with Bathsheba. Solomon disobediently collects hundreds of wives, and his sins ultimately divide God's kingdom. The Hebrew Bible is unlike other ancient documents—it does not shy away from recording the sins of its people *because it is not ultimately about the people*.

The Bible is about God, and he never sins. He never fails. He never does anything wrong or shameful. He is only ever just, holy, loving, and good. He keeps all of his promises to his people, because it is his nature to do so. He shows his great love throughout the pages of the Old Testament Scriptures by never straying from his promises to his people. The people sin against him, doubt him, and turn away from him—*but God* remains ever faithful.

They refused to obey and were not mindful of the wonders that you performed among them, but they stiffened their neck and appointed a leader to return

> *to their slavery in Egypt.*
> *But you are a God ready to forgive, gracious and*
> *merciful, slow to anger and abounding in steadfast*
> *love, and did not forsake them.*

Next:

A "But God" truth that illuminates the Incarnation in an unexpected way.

Part Two
GOD PROVIDES SALVATION FOR HIS PEOPLE

Four
GOD PROVIDES A BETTER SACRIFICE

Psalm 40:6-8, The Incarnation

I married my lovely wife, Kelly, in January 2003, and like many newly married couples, we were blessed by friends and family members with many gifts to help us start our life together. One was a DVD player—the first either of us had owned—and we felt privileged to have it. Soon, however, it began to act up. First it started skipping, then it began to eject discs for no apparent reason. Finally we replaced it; it had simply become unusable.

Unfortunately, its replacement performed even worse; it, too, needed replacing quite soon. This trend has continued. Now in our ninth year of marriage, we currently own our fourth DVD player. This hardly seems right or fair, and I have a sneaking suspicion that it is not entirely accidental.

Our woes with DVD players exemplify the dirty little secret of many consumer industries: *planned obsolescence*. Manufacturers knowingly produce items that will soon become irrelevant or useless. When this happens, consumers must buy new items. Many manufacturers thus seek not to produce items that will last but items that will need replacing at more or less predictable intervals. When we realize that a two-year-old computer has become obsolete, when the irreplaceable battery on a music player dies once and for all, or when we can date our marriages by the number of DVD players we have owned, we see planned obsolescence in action.

In the case of the sacrificial system so prominent in the Old Testament, God himself practiced a form of planned obsolescence.[8] The system was good as far as it went, but it was temporary, designed to prepare the way for something better.

No Delight in Ritual

During high school, I participated in a small-group Bible study led by a well-intentioned but somewhat biblically ignorant volunteer youth leader. Wanting us to appreciate God's grace shown through the once-for-all sacrifice of Jesus Christ, our leader contrasted it with the Old Testament sacrificial system. He told us that, under Mosaic Law, each time a person sinned, he had to sacrifice a cow in order to receive forgiveness. By contrast, Jesus' death on the cross took away that burdensome requirement. This leader was off in several key areas, but one particularly stands out—his assertion that the old covenant required animal sacrifice for personal salvation.

The Old Testament's attitude toward the sacrificial system is a bit peculiar. On the one hand, the Old Testament writers emphasize sacrifices heavily, showing the system's great importance (for example, large portions of the book of Leviticus describe the particulars of required sacrifices). But some texts seem to diminish the system's importance. Consider Psalm 40, for example, where we encounter yet another "But God" statement. David writes:

> Sacrifice and offering you have not desired, **but you** have given me an open ear. Burnt offering and sin offering you have not required. Then I said, "Behold, I have come; in the scroll of the book it is written of me: I desire to do your will, O my God; your law is within my heart." (Psalm 40:6–8)

This passage is heavily nuanced and perhaps a bit strange on the surface. It may not seem immediately obvious how this qualifies as a "But God" statement. Yet its main emphases become clear when juxtaposed with other passages of Scripture. The verses clearly contrast (highlighted by the "but God"—or, in this case, the "but you"—statement) God's lack of delight in sacrifices and his provision of an "open ear." The text goes on to specify what an "open ear" entails—it involves doing the will of God with delight, prompted by having God's Word written on the heart. When one's ears have truly opened to what God has to say, he joyfully obeys God from the heart. ("He who has ears to hear, let him hear," Jesus said in Luke 8:8.) David realized that true obedience means more than going through the motions of a sacrificial system.

Allusions to the Coming Messiah

But something deeper comes into play in this passage. Christians see Psalm 40 as a messianic psalm, and with good reason, since the New Testament cites it as such. The messianic allusions seem quite apparent, particularly in the statement "in the scroll of the book it is written of me." Jesus was the one prophesied in "the book" (that is, the Pentateuch),[9] and Psalm 40 ultimately speaks of him, not David.

The New Testament book of Hebrews develops this theme further, explicitly stating that Jesus fulfills Psalm 40:6–8. However, there is a small difference between Psalm 40 in the Old Testament and how it is quoted in Hebrews:

For since the law has but a shadow of the good

things to come instead of the true form of these realities, it can never, by the same sacrifices that are continually offered every year, make perfect those who draw near. . . . 4 For it is impossible for the blood of bulls and goats to take away sins. 5 Consequently, when Christ came into the world, he said, "Sacrifices and offerings you have not desired, *but a body you have prepared for me*; 6 in burnt offerings and sin offerings you have taken no pleasure. 7 Then I said, 'Behold, I have come to do your will, O God, as it is written of me in the scroll of the book.'" (Hebrews 10:1, 4–7)

The writer of Hebrews, under the authority of divine inspiration, sheds additional light on the meaning of Psalm 40.

First, we see that God did not delight in the old covenant sacrifices and offerings (as stated in Psalm 40) because (as explained in Hebrews 10) those sacrifices and offerings could not take away sins. So much for my former youth leader's assertion!

Second, the writer of Hebrews identifies Psalm 40:6–8 as Jesus the Son speaking to God the Father. Jesus recognizes that the Father does not delight in sacrifices, so God prepares him a body so that Jesus, the only suitable alternative, can perfectly fulfill God's will, culminating in his once-for-all sacrifice for sins on the cross.

"A body you have prepared for me" (Hebrews 10:5) sounds different than "You have given me an open ear" (Psalm 40), but the former phrasing, quoted from the Greek translation of the Old Testament, means essentially the same thing as the phrase translated differently in our versions of the psalms. Consider the original Hebrew of Psalm 40:6 translated literally: "You have dug ears for me." The Father deliberately prepared a physical body for the Son, the ears serving as a specific example (because they *listen* to the Word) of the entire body Jesus received, a body created for obedience to God.

The sacrificial system was meant to prepare the way for Jesus. And because of "planned obsolescence," the old covenant and its sacrificial system passed away. But here is where God's planned obsolescence differs from that of DVD manufacturers. The sacrificial system did not pass away only so its adherents would buy into a similar-but-slightly-improved thing all over again. It became obsolete when something infinitely better came—the incarnation of the Son of God.

One Atoning Sacrifice

Jesus was not just another man: God himself made flesh is the greatest of all of Christ's miracles, for it explains all of Jesus's other miracles. If you believe in the truth of Jesus's incarnation, all of Scripture's other teachings about him fall into place. J. I. Packer explains:

> "Tis mystery all! The Immortal dies," wrote Wesley; but there is no comparable mystery in the Immortal's resurrection. And if the immortal Son of God did really submit to taste death, it is not strange that such a death should have saving significance for a doomed race. Once we grant that Jesus was divine, it becomes unreasonable to find difficulty in any of this; it is all of a piece and hangs together completely. The Incarnation is in itself an unfathomable mystery, but it makes sense of everything else that the New Testament contains.[10]

God became flesh in order to abolish the sacrificial system. He came to provide a true sacrifice, one that could completely atone for sins. And he came in order to show what it means to have an "open ear" to the commandments of God. Jesus obeyed perfectly, his merits completely righteous. That righteousness provides a way for sinners to stand before their holy God, to make it so that "in him we might become the righteousness of God" (2 Corinthians 5:21).

The sacrificial system in the Old Testament had many purposes. First, it showed that a better sacrifice would come—one that would not require repetition.

Second, it showed that, more than empty sacrificial forms, God desired a pure heart and an "open ear." Both of these purposes were completely realized in Jesus, who by his obedience became our perfect righteousness and by his death became our perfect sacrifice.

Before Jesus came into the world, he had a conversation of sorts with God the Father, explaining why he would come. Through the inspiration of the Holy Spirit, Psalm 40 records this conversation for our benefit. In it, we see that the sacrificial system, in an example of God's planned obsolescence, would be replaced by something far better—by God made flesh, with the Word of God both in his ear and on his heart.

> *Sacrifice and offering you have not desired, but you have given me an open ear. . . . "Behold, I have come; in the scroll of the book it is written of me: I desire to do your will, O my God; your law is within my heart."*

Next:
A "But God" statement that brings perspective to the whole of Scripture.

Five

GOD DEMONSTRATES HIS LOVE FOR HIS PEOPLE

Romans 5:8, The Cross

The death of Boromir strikes me as one of the more touching scenes in the *Lord of the Rings* movie trilogy. Having received mortal wounds in a valiant attempt to save two hobbits who, like Boromir himself, are members of the Fellowship of the Ring, Boromir lies dying in the forest until Aragorn, the heroic king-in-waiting, finds him. Boromir apologizes to Aragorn for his earlier attempt to steal the magical ring that the Fellowship aims to destroy. Then, with his dying words, he pays his proper allegiance, saying, "I would have followed you, my brother . . . my captain . . . my king."

Boromir's actions were ultimately noble, good,

and right. He died for his weaker companions, who had become his friends. In this light, however, it becomes rather obvious that Boromir would never have laid down his life for his enemies (Sauron, the orcs, or other evil inhabitants of Middle Earth). Nor would anyone have expected him to do so. Only God lays down his life for his enemies.

We see this incredible love of God on display in Romans, which contains perhaps the best-known "But God" statement in all of Scripture.

> *But God* shows his love for us in that while we were still sinners, Christ died for us. (Romans 5:8)

This verse is often cited as a stand-alone concept, effectively rendering the first word irrelevant. Clearly, however, Paul intended that "but" to have significant meaning. The word at the beginning of the verse obviously connects to what came previously. Specifically, Paul uses the word to contrast two types of love, showing that God's love is infinitely greater.

Romans 5:6–8 provides the context for this "But God" statement: "For while we were still weak, at the right time Christ died for the ungodly. For one will scarcely die for a righteous person—though perhaps for a good person one would dare even to die—but God shows his love for us in that while we were still sinners, Christ died for us." God proved the magnificence of his love because his Son died for his enemies—for those who hated, opposed, and fought against him.

Feeble Human Love

In most English Bibles, we read that "perhaps for a good person one would dare to die," but the Greek text comes across as slightly different. The phrase "a good person" contains not an indefinite article ("a") but a definite article ('the"), so that the phrase literally translated reads "*the* good person." Charles Hodge describes this person as "so good as to be characterized and known as *the* good."[11] Paul writes that if there were such a man as this, maybe someone would be willing to die for him.

However, this analysis of human nature may be overly generous. After all, would anyone actually die for such a man? There *was* a man who could be defined as "*the* good man," the one who had his ear perfectly opened to the Father's will, and who obeyed it all the time. Indeed, Scripture refers to him as "Jesus Christ the righteous One" (1 John 2:1, HCSB). Absolutely perfect in every way, Jesus did only what benefited humanity. He exemplified the good in a way never seen before or since. He embodied the epitome of what a person ought to be. Not only morally correct and upright, he had no motives but love and truth and unswerving devotion to God the Father. Jesus Christ was in every way *the* good man. But nobody offered to die for him when he walked the earth.

On numerous occasions, Jesus told his disciples that he would die (e.g., Matthew 16:21) to "give his life as a ransom for many" (Matthew 20:28). But the apostles kept strangely silent about returning the favor. Peter showed a willingness to kill for Jesus (John 18:10), and at times some seemed willing to die with him (Luke 22:33, John 11:16), but never did any of Jesus' disciples offer their lives to *save* his. So when Paul says, "perhaps for *the* good man one would dare even to die," we should note that this did not happen. Truly, human love is feeble.

Furthermore, Jesus had willingly come to die for people not just *limited* in love but operating as outright enemies of God. In Romans 1 and 2, Paul proves repeatedly, in vivid language, that man opposes God, and as a result "the wrath of God is revealed from heaven against all ungodliness and unrighteousness of men, who by their unrigh- teousness suppress the truth" (Romans 1:18). The unrighteous flout God's law, but even those who appear to obey it suffer from inward corruption (2:12–29).

Paul summarizes man's condition in Romans

5:6–10 with four increasingly severe words: *weak*, *ungodly*, *sinners*, and *enemies*. Someone weak and helpless might at least seem pitiable, but the apostle moves on to describe the weak as also God's sinful enemies, so any such pity evaporates. We have nothing left to commend man to God. Sin has corrupted mankind, and we cannot save ourselves.

An Act of Divine Love, Not Just a Display

The cross is therefore tremendously important. On the cross, we see the greatest act of love ever demonstrated, its effects reverberating down through history and permanently altering the lives of those who believe. The importance of the cross will never diminish. In heaven, Scripture tells us, the majestic beings around the throne of God worship by saying, "Worthy is the Lamb who was slain, to receive power and wealth and wisdom and might and honor and glory and blessing!" (Revelation 5:12) When the love of God is extolled, both in heaven and on earth, the sacrifice of Christ on the cross is always the focal point, for there God showed his love in the most real and powerful way imaginable—by dying for those who hate him.

But the cross did not simply *display* love. On the cross, Jesus performed a real, tangible, beneficial *action* on our behalf. Though we are by nature children of wrath, Jesus died in order to achieve something for us. He "died for our sins" (1 Corinthians 15:3), so that we can be "justified by his blood" and "saved by him from the wrath of God" (Romans 5:9).

Perhaps no writer in Scripture says it better than the prophet Isaiah, despite the fact that he preceded Christ by centuries: "Surely he has borne our griefs and carried our sorrows; yet we esteemed him stricken, smitten by God, and afflicted. But he was wounded for our transgressions; he was crushed for our iniquities; upon him was the chastisement that brought us peace, and with his stripes we are healed" (Isaiah 53:4–5). Scripture plainly and clearly teaches that Jesus died in our place, as our substitute, taking from God the punishment for our sins.

Tragically, however, one increasingly influential and deeply disturbing trend in Christianity presents the cross as nothing more than a *dramatization* of God's great love for us.[12] By limiting the cross to a display of love, this approach says that Christ's work on our behalf had nothing to do with *payment* for sins. It sees the doctrine of Christ dying on our behalf to take the punishment we actually deserve as barbaric and medieval. One writer said that the Father sending the Son to suffer for our sakes would amount to "cosmic child abuse."[13] Such writers think that the Father can forgive us just because he wants to. No price needs to be paid; God can simply cancel our debt out of love and compassion. This places far more faith in a politically correct approach to ethics than it does in the words of Scripture and the character of God we see displayed on its pages.

Certainly, the cross displays God's love for us like nothing else. But the event that took place that day was deeply layered and magnificently rich, encompassing but going far beyond a mere display of love.

In fact, to claim that the cross was exclusively a display of God's love for us makes no sense. To die for someone without actually achieving anything is not noble but pointless. The late theologian Roger Nicole wrote that, "Mother Teresa showed her love for the outcasts of India by sharing in their plight. It would not have added anything to her expression of it to throw herself in the Ganges shouting, 'See how much I love you.'"[14] Jesus' death on the cross was nothing like that. On the cross, Jesus performed the ultimate act of love, and that act genuinely accomplished something—the Son of God absorbed the wrath of God on our behalf, taking our guilt away and enabling us to receive Christ's perfect righteousness credited to us, so that we might be presented before him as righteous.

Salvation Is of the Lord

This great truth of the gospel is the reason why the "But God" of Romans 5:8 gets quoted so often. But, again, we understand the verse much better when we understand why the word *but* appears there in the first place. It contrasts God's perfect love with the imperfect love of humans. It shows that apart from God's categorically and qualitatively superior love for us, we have no hope of salvation. It shows what we have already seen Scripture continually showing—that salvation is of the Lord, something only he can achieve.

Some say "God helps those who help themselves," but the Bible says the exact opposite: God helps the helpless. God helps those who, left to themselves, would die in their sins. He even helps those who hate him and who, by nature, continually oppose him. He does this because he is *not like us*. By nature, he is "merciful and gracious, slow to anger, and abounding in steadfast love and faithfulness" (Exodus 34:6).

The "But God" statement of Romans 5:8 resonates consistently with every previous "But God" statement in Scripture. It shows God's grace and initiative in saving his people. In fact, this "But God" statement makes sense of all the previous ones we have studied. God saved Noah from the flood but did not do away with Noah's sins (see Genesis 9:20–21). He saved a people for himself but dealt continually with their idolatrous sins. Even God's gift of Jesus as God's perfect righteousness did not do away with the problem of sin. But the cross did. And we praise God for this glorious truth:

> My sin, oh the bliss of this glorious thought!
> My sin, not in part but the whole,
> Is nailed to the cross, and I bear it no more,
> Praise the Lord, praise the Lord, O my soul![15]

> *But God shows his love for us in that while we were still sinners, Christ died for us.*

Next:

The "But God" statement without which Christ's death on the cross would be meaningless.

Six

GOD RAISES JESUS FROM THE DEAD

Acts 13:30, The Resurrection

A middle school student once asked me, "What is the worst sin?" I think he wanted to know which sins he should avoid and which might be okay. Intending to direct the conversation elsewhere, I answered, "The worst sin ever was the crucifixion of Jesus Christ."

In the previous chapter, we saw that Paul wrote in Romans 5 that one might perhaps die for *the* ideal man. In history, however, when the ideal man lived among us, not only did no one offer to die for him, we killed him instead. I am convinced that was the worst act human hands ever committed.

The question of who killed Jesus has often sparked contentious debate. Throughout history, many have held the Jews responsible for Jesus' death, leading to instances of anti-Semitism. The gospel accounts, however, clearly show that the Jews suggested the crucifixion and the Gentiles carried it out—thus, in a sense, implicating all of humanity.

Of course, no group of mere humans could overcome and kill the Son of God against God's will. Therefore, it must be *God himself* who delivered Jesus over to crucifixion. Jesus told Pontius Pilate, "You would have no authority over me at all unless it had been given you from above" (John 19:11a), and Isaiah tells us that "it was the will of the LORD to crush him" (Isaiah 53:10). John Piper writes, "The ultimate answer to the question, Who crucified Jesus? is: God did. It is a staggering thought. Jesus was his Son. And the suffering was unsurpassed. But the whole message of the Bible leads to this conclusion."[16]

A Real Death, Real Burial, and Real Resurrection

The death of Jesus was a very real event. No mere act, he really died. Therefore, statements in Scripture about Christ's death are frequently followed by statements about his burial (i.e., 1 Corinthians 15:3–4). His burial showed that his death actually happened.[17]

During his first missionary journey, Paul spoke to a group of Jews in Antioch, attempting to persuade them that Jesus is the Messiah. At one point, he summarized the sinful steps that led to the death of Christ, saying, "And though they found in him no guilt worthy of death, they asked Pilate to have him executed. And when they had carried out all that was written of him, they took him down from the tree and laid him in a tomb" (Acts 13:28–29). Under the sovereign hand of God, humanity carried out its most reprehensible sin. Thereafter, the perfect Son of God lay buried in a tomb, capitally punished for a crime he didn't commit.

Of course, that did not end the story. Another "But God" moment would come. In the next verse of Paul's speech, he announces it.

❚ *But God* raised him from the dead. (Acts 13:30)

By killing and burying Jesus, humanity had attempted to turn the world order upside down, ripping the keys of death from God's hands and using them against him. For a moment, the attempt appeared to have succeeded. But God overcame the sinful acts of men. (He always had these under his control anyway; hence, Paul emphasized in Acts 13 that everything came to pass according to Scripture.) God raised Jesus from the dead, triumphing over man's disobedience and lust for power.

Sermons recorded in the book of Acts share

this as a common theme. Peter often made similar statements, at times phrasing them in an especially pointed manner: "You killed Jesus, but God raised him" (e.g., Acts 2:23–24; 3:15; 4:10; 5:30; 10:39–40). The resurrection of Jesus leaves no doubt that God retained control the entire time. The cross did not derail God's plan, for if God can overcome death itself, he certainly could have prevented the crucifixion to begin with. The resurrection shows God's supreme ability to take a situation intended by mankind for evil and turn it into the ultimate good.

The resurrection of Jesus was as real as his death. Thus, Paul stated that after Jesus' resurrection, "for many days he appeared to those who had come up with him from Galilee to Jerusalem, who are now his witnesses to the people" (13:31). Paul emphasizes that these people knew Jesus well and could confirm that he did not die in body but rise again in spirit only. On the contrary, in his resurrected state he walked, spoke, and ate (Luke 24:15, 38–39, 42–43), just as before his crucifixion. Thus, through the cross God did not merely achieve some sort of "moral victory"; he completely undid mankind's attempt to usurp his sovereignty. In doing so, God (as he always does) achieved much good for his people.

We often treat the resurrection as merely an epilogue to the great story of Jesus' sacrifice on the cross. Many criticized Mel Gibson's movie *The*

Passion of the Christ for taking just that approach. Given that the film purposed to portray the crucifixion and not the resurrection, this might not have been the most valid criticism, yet the movie's emphasis does reflect the perspective of many Christians. The cross gets all the attention, with hardly anything left over for the resurrection. This is unfortunate, because a cross without a resurrection is a cross stripped of power, devoid of meaning, and unable to save.

A Statement and a Foretaste

We could consider many reasons why the resurrection is of great importance. We will focus on two.

A statement. In the resurrection, God made a major statement: humanity is not a doomed race, for the fall can be reversed. The Messiah has come and he has completed his work, proving once and for all that physical death can be overcome and sin can be forgiven.

The resurrection proves that sin and death (products of the fall) could actually be defeated — in real life and not just in theory. Christ's resurrection dramatically showed that through the promised Messiah, God had triumphed over Satan and would do so again. Jesus' resurrection confirmed that on the cross, God had destroyed the power of the devil (Hebrews 2:14-15). The resurrection also foreshadows Jesus' second coming, "when he delivers the kingdom to God the Father after destroying every rule and every authority and power. For he must reign until he has put all his enemies under his feet" (1 Corinthians 15:24-25).

In his Acts 13 sermon, Paul showed that Psalm 16 refers to the Messiah and not to David, and he demonstrated how Christ's resurrection fulfilled that psalm (Acts 13:32–39). The resurrection declared once and for all that Jesus was the divine Son. Paul would later write in Romans that Jesus "was *declared to be the Son of God* in power according to the Spirit of holiness *by his resurrection from the dead*" (1:4).

So the resurrection served as much more than an epilogue to the story of Jesus. It gave a victory cry, an eternal declaration, a triumphant shout in which God broke the chains of death and emphatically declared Jesus to be his divine Son, the one spoken of in times past as coming to defeat sin.

A foretaste. By the resurrection, God also provided a foretaste of what awaits his people. If the cross reminds us of our sins and what God has saved us *from*, the resurrection previews our future and what God saves us *to*. Paul makes clear in 1 Corinthians 15 that Christ's resurrection models what we who believe in him will one day experience: "But in fact Christ has been raised from the dead, the firstfruits of those who have fallen asleep. . . . For as in Adam all die, so also in Christ shall all be made alive. But each in his own order: Christ the firstfruits, then at his coming those who belong to Christ" (1 Corinthians 15:20, 22–23). "Firstfruits" is an agricultural reference to the earliest crop harvested; the firstfruits showed what the remainder of the crop would be like. If the firstfruits were good, a farmer could expect his entire harvest to be good, but if not, he would know that he ought to prepare for a lean year. In the same manner, Jesus has been raised as our firstfruits, showing what our own resurrection from the dead will be like.

The resurrection of Jesus was not like any other resurrection in Scripture. For instance, when Jesus raised Lazarus from the dead, he appeared in a healed version of his original body, and his resurrection was not permanent—he died again. But when Jesus rose from the dead, it was to life eternal in a glorified body. Instead of eventually returning to the grave, Jesus ascended to heaven (Acts 1:9–11). Those of us who believe will follow in the same manner one day. No longer will we have perishable, dishonorable, and weak bodies; we will enjoy imperishable, glorious, and strong bodies (1 Corinthians 15:43). We will never experience the awful sting of death again: "When the perishable puts on the imperishable, and the mortal puts on immortality, then shall come to pass the saying that is written: 'Death is swallowed up in victory.' 'O death, where is your victory? O death, where is your sting?'" (1 Corinthians 15:54–55).

It is a terrible thing to watch a loved one die, especially from a debilitating illness—to see the human body wither away, strength failing, life diminishing. But "at the last trumpet" (1 Corinthians 15:52), such things will cease for God's children. The last enemy God will destroy is death. *What he did for Jesus, he will do for all who follow Jesus.* We all long for this glorification, the final marvelous step in our salvation, and because of the resurrection of Jesus, we can wait expectantly for it. Because Jesus died for our sins, we will live forever with God. And because he rose again, we have received a glimpse of that day when death will die forever.

Praise God that Jesus did not gain a merely theoretical victory over sin, but that his resurrection proved his victory was genuine and powerful. Praise God that Jesus was not among the many pseudo-messiahs of human history, but that his resurrection proved he was the real deal. Praise God that because of his resurrection, we have a better future to antici-pate. And praise God that when man committed the worst sin in human history, God turned it into eternal benefit for all who believe.

But God raised him from the dead.

Next:

The "But God" statement that helps explain the mystery of God's election.

Part Three

GOD APPLIES SALVATION TO HIS PEOPLE

Seven
GOD CHOOSES THE FOOLISH AND THE WEAK

1 Corinthians 1:27, Election

In recent years American evangelicals have seen a resurgence of what we simply call Reformed theology. While this resurgence encompasses a broad spectrum of denominations and theological traditions, it has focused on one key doctrine: the sovereignty of God in salvation.

Reformed (or Calvinist) theology expands on the idea that God is sovereign in salvation through a series of theological tenets knows as "the doctrines of grace." Although this is not a new phrase (the Puritans used it regularly), it too has experienced a bit of a comeback within modern Calvinist movements. Adherents of Reformed theology are drawn to it because it magnifies the role of God's grace in the salvation of sinners.

The doctrines of grace themselves center around the key doctrine of unconditional election. While sometimes controversial, this doctrine does seem clearly taught in Scripture. Wayne Grudem defines unconditional election as, "An act of God before creation in which he chooses some people to be saved, not on account of any foreseen merit in them, but only because of his sovereign good pleasure."[18]

In simple terms, the doctrines of grace, especially the doctrine of unconditional election, teach that there must be a "But God" event in every sinner's life, for no sinner would ever choose God if not for God's prior choice of him or her.

An Unlikely Wisdom

Nowhere in Scripture is this expressed more clearly than in the epistles of Paul.[19] At the beginning of his first letter to the Corinthians, Paul expounds the glory of the cross, which is "folly to those who are perishing, but to us who are being saved it is the power of God" (1 Corinthians 1:18). He goes on to say that the cross does not gel with the wisdom of the world, which regards it as the "foolishness of God"; this "foolishness," however, "is wiser than men" (v 25).

The remarkable message of the cross is that one Jesus of Nazareth, a first-century Jewish carpenter, quite ordinary by material standards, was no mere man but the divine Son of God. When he suffered an unjust death on a Roman cross, it came by divine design so that his death could pay for sins. His death, of course, did not signal an end, for he was raised again, triumphing over death itself and paving the way for the resurrection of those who believe in him. This foolish-sounding message did not win over the majority of the elite minds in Paul's day. Nor has it done so in our day.

Part of the reason God's plan appears foolish to human wisdom is because of those whom God frequently chooses for salvation. Paul tells the Corinthian church, "For consider your calling, brothers: not many of you were wise according to worldly standards, not many were powerful, not many were of noble birth" (v 26). The Corinthian believers were not the aristocrats of society. They were not the academics, the wealthy and powerful, nor even what we might call "good," having been called out of a perverted and pornographic pagan society. On its own, Paul's statement seems almost degrading; he essentially says, "You had nothing going for you; you were nobodies."

What Paul says next turns everything on its head.

> ***But God*** chose what is foolish in the world to shame the wise; God chose what is weak in the world to shame the strong; God chose what is

low and despised in the world, even things that are not, to bring to nothing things that are, so that no human being might boast in the presence of God (1 Corinthians 1:27–29).

This statement touches on the glorious truth of unconditional election: God does not choose anyone because of merit or status but simply to display his power and glory by demonstrating grace. As Paul writes elsewhere: "he chose us in him before the foundation of the world, that we should be holy and blameless before him. In love he predestined us for adoption through Jesus Christ, according to the purpose of his will, to the praise of his glorious grace, with which he has blessed us in the Beloved" (Ephesians 1:4–6).

God has always worked to maximize his glory by choosing the weakest and least remarkable members of society. When he called a nation to himself, he did not choose a powerful kingdom but an oppressed band of slaves. When Jesus walked the earth and called disciples to himself, he did not select cultural leaders but everyday fishermen and other simple people. The first-century church grew especially quickly because of the large number of slaves and other outcasts, like those in Corinth, who came to faith in Christ. Even today, it is relatively unusual to find a committed Christian in a high-status segment of society such as entertainment, sports, politics, or academia.[20] God delights in choosing outcasts, those who see that they cannot help themselves.

We cannot, therefore, attribute the growth of the Christian church, particularly in its earliest days, to any human power, ingenuity, or methodology, but only to the working of the almighty hand of God. The gospel of Jesus Christ made an explosive impact throughout the world (and continues to do so today) without the help of society's leaders. The saving power of God made it happen.

A Like Grace

One clear and practical implication of the doctrine of unconditional election is this: those who believe it should be exceptionally gracious people. Should we not be humbled by the fact that we did nothing to save ourselves? Should we not be humbled by God's manner of choosing those of little importance to the world?

If we believe the Bible's teaching that we have been saved simply because God chose to save us, shouldn't this stir us up to help those in need, even those who do not deserve it? Should it not make us kind and patient toward others, and far less tempted to be critical of those who do not "measure up"? Should we not be the most loving, encouraging, forgiving, and compassionate people on earth? The doctrine of election calls us to teach others the truth in love, not flee them in fear, not reject or look down on them in pride.

But this is not always the case, is it? Some who come to a biblical understanding of God's sovereignty in salvation become arrogant about it. We can feel superior to those who do not see Scripture the way we do. On the one hand, we can claim that all our spiritual understanding of the Bible is a gift of God's grace, and on the other hand we can criticize and belittle others for holding a different understanding of that same Bible. This attitude should never be. Calvinism properly understood kills pride; it never creates it. What pride can we derive from the doctrine of total depravity, which holds that man is dead in his sin (Ephesians 2:1) and therefore cannot please God or choose to follow him? What superiority can we feel over our complete inability to save ourselves? How can we esteem ourselves above all others when we hold to a system that explicitly teaches us to esteem others as better than ourselves (Philippians 2:3) and to esteem God above all? Yet this happens more often than many care to admit, and it is especially prevalent—at times, shamefully prevalent—on the Internet.

I do not want to overstate my point. For the most part, the Christians I know who hold to the doctrines of grace are some of the most gracious people I have met. They recognize the grace God has shown in saving them, and they seek to extend grace to others. They encourage others instead of tearing them down. They teach others instead of belittling them. They give to others instead of accumulating things for themselves. These traits should mark one who knows the grace of God in all its biblical glory.[21]

But these traits did not characterize the Corinthians when Paul wrote his first letter to them. Divisions had popped up among them, as some claimed superiority over others because they followed certain leaders. Paul wrote, "each one of you says, 'I follow Paul,' or 'I follow Apollos,' or 'I follow Cephas,' or 'I follow Christ'" (1:12). Following men can be well and good (just as we may "follow" Martin Luther, John Calvin, John Wesley, or any number of Christian leaders, living or dead), but the Corinthians' arrogance in doing so was tearing the church apart.

To combat this problem and call the Corinthians back to unity in the church through humility, Paul chose to emphasize the doctrine of election. "Consider your calling," he wrote to them. By this he did not refer to anyone's occupation or station in life. He referred, rather, to how God had called them to Christ. He reminded them that they had done nothing to save themselves. In fact, had human wisdom been used to select people to build God's church, Paul suggested, the Corinthians would have fallen near the bottom of the list. They would have received no salvation—they never would have become a part of Christ's church—if not for God's initiative toward them.

"But God" enabled them to come to faith. "But God" brought them from darkness to light. "But God" saved their souls. This truth should have humbled them and destroyed their arrogant faction-alism. It should do the same in us.

Power from God, Not Sinners

Just as God's unilateral action and initiative was the unique and indispensable key

- to preserving humanity in the days of Noah,
- to God selecting a nation for himself,
- to appointing Jesus to die for sinners, and
- to Christ resurrecting from the dead…

… so it is the key to applying salvation to the lives of sinful individuals. Paul wrote of this truth to the Colossians: "you were also raised with him through faith in the powerful working of God, who raised him from the dead. And you, who were dead in your trespasses and the uncircumcision of your flesh, God made alive together with him" (2:12–13). The same power that raised Christ from the dead raises believers from spiritual death to life. It comes from God, from beginning to end, not from sinners.

We must never forget the doctrine of unconditional election, for it reminds us of the unfathomable grace of God, who chose us only *for* his glory and *by* his grace. It tells us that God did not wait for us to draw near to him, but acted from eternity past to draw us to himself. It motivates us to share the gospel, knowing that God has chosen others who have yet to respond in faith. And it keeps us humble.

If we forget the truth of unconditional election, we run the risk of turning into the Christian equivalent of spoiled children—those who pride themselves in how much they have even though they did not earn it. The doctrine of election teaches us that from beginning to end, salvation is all of grace. If it were based on our ability, none of us would be saved.

Our God often chooses people of little importance. But that humbling act of intervention makes all the difference, for the one who has been drawn to faith in Christ has more wisdom than the most erudite scholar, more power than the most important leader, and more privilege than the richest billionaire.

But God chose what is foolish in the world to shame the wise.

Next:

The "But God" statement that marks our transition from death to life.

Eight
GOD BRINGS LIFE OUT OF DEATH

Ephesians 2:4, Salvation

Why does God love anyone?

Several years ago, several of my friends and I read a particular Christian book. The book was commendable in some ways, but one statement in particular did not sit well with me. The author wrote: "I think the difference in my life came when I realized, after reading the Gospels, that Jesus didn't just love me out of principle; he didn't just love me because it was the right thing to do. Rather, there was something inside me that caused him to love me."[22]

Does Scripture teach this? With his all-seeing eye, does God gaze deep into our souls and find there a precious kernel of something that irresistibly draws out of him a deep love for fallen man? In this chapter, we will focus on the "But God" statement in Scripture that covers probably a wider scope than any other, while also addressing this vital issue.

A Startling Contrast

In describing exactly what happens when the grace of God intersects with the life of a sinner, Paul draws a number of stark distinctions between the believer and the unbeliever. To appreciate the full force of the text, we must read at least the following passage.

> And you were dead in the trespasses and sins ² in which you once walked, following the course of this world, following the prince of the power of the air, the spirit that is now at work in the sons of disobedience— ³ among whom we all once lived in the passions of our flesh, carrying out the desires of the body and the mind, and were by nature children of wrath, like the rest of mankind. ⁴ *But God*, being rich in mercy, because of the great love with which he loved us, ⁵ even when we were dead in our trespasses, made us alive together with Christ—by grace you have been saved— ⁶ and raised us up with him and seated us with him in the heavenly places in Christ Jesus, ⁷ so that in the coming ages he might show the immeasurable riches of his grace in kindness toward us in Christ Jesus. (Ephesians 2:1–7)

Notice the startling and vast contrast between verses 1–3 and verses 4–7: the life of the unbeliever consists of death and sin while the believer experiences life and grace, and the difference-maker is "But God." When a believer comes to God in faith, believing in Jesus for the forgiveness of sins, that person literally moves from death to life, something that only God himself can accomplish.

But Paul's description of the differences between the believer and the unbeliever does not end with these verses. He draws even more contrasts in verses 11–22. If we combine the contents of these two texts (Ephesians 2:1–7 and 11–22), we see the following differences between the unsaved person and the saved person.

Unsaved

- Dead in trespasses and sins (v 1)
- Following the course of the world, the Devil, and a spirit of disobedience (v 2)
- Living in the passions of the flesh (v 3)
- Carrying out the desires of the body and of the mind (v 3)
- By nature children of wrath (v 3)
- Separated from the people of God and from Christ (vv 11–12)
- Strangers to God's covenants (v 12)
- Without hope, without God (v 12)
- Strangers and aliens in this world (v 19)

Saved

- Recipients of God's mercy and love, and of the peace of Christ (v 4, 14)
- Made alive, and made a part of the people of God (v 5, 13)
- Raised with Christ (v 6)
- Seated with Christ in the heavenly places (v 6)
- Set to receive grace throughout eternity (v 7)
- Reconciled to God (v 16)
- No hostility between God and man (v 16)
- Access in the Spirit to God the Father (v 18)
- Citizens and members of God's house (v 19)
- Built upon Christ and his Word (v 20)
- Growing into a holy temple in the Lord (v 21)
- Built into a dwelling place for God (v 22)

Nothing can transform the first set of characteristics into the second except God. So it is not surprising that after Paul describes unbelievers in some depth, we find the words "But God" in verse 4. The unsaved, whether aware of it or not, are in a desperately tragic situation which they cannot change. Yet the story does not end there. God does not leave people, created in his image, entirely without hope. He acts in order to save them, and he does so because of his own nature: "But God, being rich in mercy, because of the great love with which he loved us, even when we were dead in our trespasses . . ." God saves for one reason, because he is merciful and loving. His bright character set against the dark backdrop of humanity's sinfulness illuminates the incredible nature of his grace.

The God Who Loves

So does God love us because we are lovable? Quite the opposite. We all followed sin, Satan, and self. Apart from God's gracious intervention, we would have remained objects of his wrath instead of recipients of his grace. But God chose to show grace, and in doing so, he chose us.

God did this only because of who he is. Recall how he described himself to Moses: "The LORD, the LORD, a God merciful and gracious, slow to anger, and abounding in steadfast love and faithfulness, keeping steadfast love for thousands, forgiving iniquity and transgression and sin" (Exodus 34:6–7). This God is, always has been, always will be. He is merciful and loving. Therefore, he acts on our behalf, unilaterally, out of mercy rooted in love. One Bible commentator has written, "Mercy and love are revelations of God's being, not a response to something that merits love in the individual. God acts in mercy because he is that kind of God."[23]

When considering a "But God" statement in Scripture, it can help to think of what would be true if not for that statement. Sometimes this is easy — if

God had not remembered Noah in the days of the flood, the human race would have perished. Sometimes it is difficult or even impossible—we simply cannot say what biblical history would have looked like if God had chosen a people other than Israel to grace with his covenants (Deuteronomy 29:29).

We can discern our fate quite easily, however, by imagining what would be true if the "But God" statement in Ephesians 2 were not there. The list would end with the "unsaved" category. We could read no list of attributes and benefits accrued to the saved, because there would be no saved. We would all continue dead in our sins—every man, woman, and child from Adam until the end of our race. We would have no hope. We would remain children of wrath forever, having nothing worthy of redemption within us, and no amount of human effort could change this.

The God Who Intervenes

If any would be saved, ever, God had to intervene. He had to act first. And he did: "For by grace you have been saved through faith. And this is not your own doing; it is the gift of God, not a result of works, so that no one may boast" (Ephesians 2:8–9). God's grace is the necessary first cause, and the sustaining power, of every aspect and moment of our salvation.

Yes, we believe in him and so receive the remarkable benefits described in Scripture, but even the ability to believe is a gift from him. It is "not [our] own doing." Just as Paul told the Corinthians, so he tells the Ephesians—God chose them *before* they chose him.[24]

We see God's intervention all over the pages of Scripture, nowhere more than in the salvation of those who have believed in Jesus for the forgiveness of sins. "But God" paves the way for every aspect of the believer's faith in Christ.

I recently found myself sucked into watching the 1980s movie *Brewster's Millions*, in which a washed-up minor-league ballplayer goes through a series of horrendous (yet occasionally humorous) ordeals to secure an inheritance from a distant relative. This relative has put a number of restrictions in place so that Brewster, the lead character, will likely not receive the inheritance. He has made inheriting the money a great challenge.

God is not at all like this relative. He places no arbitrary stipulations on us receiving his glorious inheritance, and he carries no malicious intent toward us. God did not consider within himself how to devise a series of challenges by which, with hard work and sincerity, we could make our way toward him or conceivably earn his favor. God's requirements do not arise out of any desire to oppress us or make us jump through hoops. They arise out of the simple fact that, in order for him to find us acceptable and thus worthy of his inheritance, we must be holy.

Our God is absolute moral perfection—perfection so all-encompassing, so beyond the scope of our wildest imaginations, so extensive that it will fascinate us and draw from us the deepest worship for all eternity. In a sense, God requires something quite simple of us: we too, like him, must be pure and holy. Unlike Brewster's relative, God does not impose requirements difficult for an average person to meet: rather, they are *impossible*. In order to meet God's requirements for salvation on our own, we must be as holy and good and righteous as God himself.

Enter Christ, the Lamb slain from the foundation of the world. By his sacrifice and his payment for sins on our behalf, God counts us as holy—*and this alone qualifies us for the inheritance*. Through the gospel, God not only secures the inheritance for us, he meets every stipulation on our behalf and brings us to the place where we can receive the inheritance. He acts decisively at every point along the way to insure our good. Why? Because he is merciful and loving. He transforms spiritually dead and utterly sinful people into living followers of Jesus Christ.

A Crown to Claim

The "But God" of Ephesians 2:4 describes amazing accomplishments for our sake. It shows what happens when all that God has achieved on our behalf (sending Christ, atoning for sin, conquering death, choosing us in him) actually comes into our lives. God did not send Jesus to accomplish an abstraction, something with no practical impact. He did it so that he could actually apply Jesus' work to our lives. Everything we have in Christ—forgiveness of sins, membership in the body of Christ, fellowship with God himself—is the gift of God as a direct result of Jesus' life, death, and resurrection.

One of my favorite hymns is Charles Wesley's "And Can It Be That I Should Gain?" This great song poetically states what it looks like for the "But God" of Ephesians 2 to invade the life of the believer. Wesley wrote:

Long my imprisoned spirit lay,
Fast bound in sin and nature's night;
Thine eye diffused a quickening[25] ray—
I woke, the dungeon flamed with light;
My chains fell off, my heart was free,
I rose, went forth, and followed Thee.

Every believer shares this same experience—whether converted young or old, whether saved from a life of horrendous evil or one of prideful moralism. All must be brought to life by God's Spirit, have their sins taken away, and follow Jesus. This is what it means to be a Christian. When this happens in a believer's life, all the benefits of Ephesians 2 belong to him:

No condemnation now I dread;
Jesus, and all in Him, is mine;
Alive in Him, my living Head,
And clothed in righteousness divine,
Bold I approach th' eternal throne,
And claim the crown, through Christ my own.

God gives us this crown, purchased for us by Christ, through the undeserved gift of faith. He has done everything to make this happen. And he will do everything to keep these blessings for us.

But God, being rich in mercy, because of the great love with which he loved us . . . made us alive together with Christ.

Next:
The "But God" statement that assures our perseverance in the faith.

Nine
GOD'S FIRM FOUNDATION STANDS

2 Timothy 2:19, Perseverance

In his last known letter, Paul wrote to his young protégé Timothy, who was pastoring in Ephesus amid false teachers and other enemies of the faith. These men were drawing members of Timothy's congregation away, so Paul wrote to encourage Timothy with the truth of God's grace toward his children, and to exhort him to stand firm, to preach the Word of God with boldness and clarity, and to live a holy life.

Concerning false teachers in Ephesus, Paul wrote:

> They are upsetting the faith of some. [19] *But God's* firm foundation stands, bearing this seal: "The Lord knows those who are his," and "Let everyone who names the name of the Lord depart from iniquity." (2 Timothy 2:18b–19)

With these words, Paul acknowledged that the false teachers did have an impact—they confused some Ephesian believers by declaring that the resurrection of the faithful had already happened (verse 18). Moreover, their influence was spreading, and Timothy undoubtedly found this discouraging.

But Paul reassured Timothy. With the words "But God," Paul began to lay out reasons Timothy could know for sure that the faith of true believers would not be undermined—a reassurance based not on Timothy's abilities or righteousness, but on God's grace alone.

Even though some had been lured away from the faith, Paul said, the faith of the elect had not been shaken; indeed, nothing can shake their faith. Those drawn to genuine faith in Christ, who count the cost and follow him, cannot be taken away from him. Indeed, Jesus said of his followers, "I give them eternal life, and they will never perish, and no one will snatch them out of my hand" (John 10:28). Jesus also said that in the end times false prophets would "perform great signs and wonders, so as to lead astray, if possible, even the elect" (Matthew 24:24). He used the phrase "if possible" to assure his followers that even though false prophets might attract a large following by seeming to perform great miracles, they would not ultimately deceive the elect.[26]

A Foundation Sealed by God

Paul assured Timothy that the elect under his care were safe because God had placed them on a firm foundation, sealed by God himself. Paul's metaphor alludes to "the practice of inscribing a seal on the foundation of a building in order to indicate ownership and sometimes the function of the building."[27] I have often noticed such a seal near the base of a building. The seal typically shows a set of initials or perhaps a symbol (sometimes that of the Freemasons or another group) indicating the original owner or the builder of the structure. However, most seals on the buildings where I live, not much more than a century old, function only as historical markers: they mean nothing today because the buildings have long since changed hands and/or the original owners have died. But God's seal on his elect is not temporary like this. In fact, Paul mentions two permanent, unchanging seals in this passage.

The seal of being known. The first seal, "The Lord knows those who are his," alludes to Numbers 16:5.

When the Israelite spies returned from scouting out the Promised Land, the people turned away from God's command to conquer the land because of their fear of the land's strong inhabitants. God judged the nation by refusing to allow that generation to enter the land. He told them they would wander in the wilderness for forty more years and die there, and that only their children would inherit Canaan. Nevertheless, the people went into battle against their enemies, only to lose miserably because they did not have God's blessing upon them.

This was a low point in the history of Israel, and the community found itself in disarray. Into this uncertainty stepped three respected men, Korah, Dathan, and Abiram. They questioned Moses' leadership and claimed that everyone should have an equal share in leading the people. Moses said that God knew which people truly belonged to him, and that God would decide the dispute. God indeed acted quickly, causing the earth to open and swallow Korah and his men (Numbers 16:31–33). God showed that he knew those who were his.

Paul alluded to this statement by Moses to show that God knows his own within the church and will not let them be led astray. This truth still stands. He will not let his elect be stripped away from him. Once known by God, we are known forever. The same intervening grace that saved us sustains us and carries us to the end.

The seal of sanctification and perseverance. The second seal, "Let everyone who names the name of the Lord depart from iniquity," does not come directly from any one biblical passage, though it may be inspired by Numbers 16:26, given the previous reference to Numbers 16. However, it is clearly a biblical command.

True believers have followed Jesus Christ not only in belief but also in repentance, turning away from sin (e.g., Acts 2:38). No believer is saved by works; this book has driven that point home again and again. Only God can save. And yet, when God saves, he does not leave sinners as they are. He gives them his Holy Spirit, and as a result, they grow in holiness. Nobody reaches perfection in this life, but all true believers depart from sin and give evidence of the fruit of the Spirit. Thus sealed by God, they do not and cannot depart from the faith.

When it seemed to Timothy as if believers were departing the faith, Paul gave him two reasons for unshakable confidence. First, God knows his own, having chosen them from before the foundation of the world, so he will not let them go. And second, those whom God has saved show evidence of that calling in their manner of life by turning from sin and persevering in faith.

God-Empowered Perseverance

These twin seals on every believer form the basis of the doctrine of the perseverance of the saints. Some prefer to call this the doctrine of eternal security, but this label does not reflect Scripture's teaching as fully as does "perseverance of the saints." Some use the doctrine of eternal security (often phrased as "Once saved, always saved") to justify their misguided belief that there is salvation for individuals who have made a profession of faith in Jesus as their Savior but have not yet bowed to him as their Lord.[28] But the label "perseverance of the saints" presents a more fully biblical picture of the believer's destiny on earth. True followers of Christ persevere in faith and holiness until the end of life.

Of course, Scripture presents the believer's ability to persevere as a gift of grace. Peter calls believers those "who by God's power are being guarded through faith for a salvation ready to be revealed in the last time" (1 Peter 1:5). Paul writes that "if we are faithless, he remains faithful—for he cannot deny himself" (2 Timothy 2:13). Paul wanted Timothy to have confidence in the perseverance of the saints, but not because of the saints themselves. Paul's confidence was in God. All of the "But God" statements we have seen so far have shown that God acts incredibly intentionally to secure salvation for his children at every possible step along the way. He would never leave it up to sinful humans to determine whether they will remain saved. There is a "But God" even in the keeping of believers until the end.

The Christian life can be very hard. It does not summon you to "Your best life now" but to respond daily to Jesus' high and holy calling: "If anyone would come after me, let him deny himself and take up his cross and follow me" (Matthew 16:24). Jesus told his disciples, "In the world you will have tribulation" (John 16:33). He promised them, "If they persecuted me, they will also persecute you" (John 15:20). Paul echoed this sentiment: "Indeed, all who desire to live a godly life in Christ Jesus will be persecuted" (2 Timothy 3:12). The Christian life is not easy, but it is worth it.

Sinful and weak as we are, it would be hard for us to remember this if God did not constantly sustain us. Though many of us in the West have experienced persecution only in milder forms (i.e., exclusion, derision, loss of promotion), many around the world have lost homes, family members, and more for the sake of Jesus Christ. These believers have endured in spite of these attacks, some of them enduring to the point of death. In the same way, some believers in the early church were imprisoned and lost their homes because of their faith, and the writer of Hebrews described their perseverance in this way: "For you had compassion on those in prison, and you joyfully accepted the plundering of your property, since you knew that you yourselves had a better possession and an abiding one" (Hebrews 10:34). How does a person maintain such an attitude amid severe perse-cution, not only accepting it but finding joy in the midst of it? Such perseverance comes only from God. It is a gift of grace.

The children of God will not lose the salvation he has secured for them. In spite of temptations, false teachings, persecutions, and any number of other things that might drag a believer away from Jesus, they will hold on to God, for he will hold on to his own. He knows them, he loves them, and he will protect them. He will not let anyone else snatch them away. He will give them a spirit of holy perseverance. When they are attacked, he will enable them through faith to hold tightly to their good confession, to cling to Jesus above all else. He will not leave them to secure themselves according to their own strength but will constantly work to secure his own.

And he will always succeed.

They are upsetting the faith of some. But God's firm foundation stands, bearing this seal: "The Lord knows those who are his," and, "Let everyone who names the name of the Lord depart from iniquity."

Ten
FINAL THOUGHTS

The phrase "But God," as it appears in Scripture, is no accident of language. It does not operate as a semantic novelty or an interesting bit of Bible trivia. Rather, the phrase has profound significance. From just the few examples touched on in this book, given their pivotal placement and world-changing import, we see at least two things: that God is entirely different from us, and that God acts in this world.

God is not like us. The "But God" statements of Scripture often follow accounts of the short-comings and sins of man. Whether the prevalent evil of humanity that led to the flood in Noah's day, the obstinacy of the Hebrews throughout the Old Testament, the defiant insistence of the Jewish leaders about crucifying Jesus, or the willingness of nominal believers to run away from the Christian faith into false teaching, mankind's sins have repeat-edly made a mess of this world. But God has been there each time, acting in spite of these sins, and using them for his own ends. The biblical story line follows man down a trail of sin to its bitter end . . . where God yet remains, only and ever good and holy and intent on his purpose.

Man sinned, *but God* was there, and he made things right. He never commits sin; he is entirely different from man.

God acts. "But God" also means that God acts. "Deism" describes the belief that God created the world, set things in motion, and then left man to fend for himself, but that view does not come from Scripture. God is history's biggest player. Whether unmistakably out in front or acting subtly behind the scenes, in each and every case God is there, working all things to his glory. Many Christians live as practical deists. We believe in God, but we often depend on ourselves to work things out in the here and now: we do not trust him to do so. But the Bible shatters such disbelief. Our God is a God who works, both for his glory and our good.

Because God has worked throughout history to accomplish salvation for us, and because he has promised to secure that salvation in us through the perseverance he bestows, we can count on him to continue working in our lives. The "But God" statements of Scripture do not represent the only times God has worked. He has worked in all believers at all times, and he continues to work today: "for it is God who works in you, both to will and to work for his good pleasure" (Philippians 2:13).

This means that we should recognize as believers that "But God" is a constant in our lives.

- We should believe like Joseph, who, after enduring trouble at the hands of his brothers, told them, "As for you, you meant evil against me, *but God* meant it for good" (Genesis 50:20).
- When we face various difficulties—sickness, hardship, poverty, arguments—we can say with Paul: "our bodies had no rest, but we were afflicted at every turn—fighting without and fear within. *But God*, who comforts the downcast, comforted us" (2 Corinthians 7:5–6).
- When we engage in ministry efforts and see God's blessing on them, we can say something like this: "I planted, Apollos watered, *but God* gave the growth" (1 Corinthians 3:6).
- When God heals us or others we know from illness or disease, we should echo Paul's sentiments about Epaphroditus: "Indeed he was ill, near to death. *But God* had mercy on him" (Philippians 2:27a).

Better Than "But Me"

One of the greatest examples of the benefits of a "But God" mindset comes in Psalm 73. The psalmist

Asaph wrestled with the difficult question of why evil people received material blessings while he, a godly man, struggled to get by. The psalm begins like this: "Truly God is good to Israel, to those who are pure in heart. But as for me, my feet had almost stumbled, my steps had nearly slipped. For I was envious of the arrogant when I saw the prosperity of the wicked" (Psalm 73:1–3).

Asaph recounts his belief in God's goodness—a belief based firmly in the biblical account (Exodus 33:19). But he admits that this confidence faltered when he relied not on the Word of God but on his own feelings and observations of the world. He came to have what we could call a "But me" attitude. He knew what God's Word said, but it did not align with his feelings and experiences, and he nearly discarded it.

As the psalm moves on, Asaph tells how he learned the truth of God's holiness and justice, which brought him back into a full and robust faith. Then he utters one of the greatest "But God" statements in all of Scripture, saying, "My flesh and my heart may fail, ***but God*** is the strength of my heart and my portion forever" (Psalm 73:26). His faith led him into deeper devotion to God and gave him an increased desire to share God with others (v 28). He gained this attitude by keeping in mind the "But God" truth in his own life. No matter how difficult his life became,

God remained his portion that no one could take away from him, and he could rejoice in that.

When Asaph had a "But me" attitude, focusing on his problems and his inability to fix things, he doubted God's goodness and became bitter. When he gained a "But God" attitude, he received peace, joy, contentment, and zeal. What a difference it makes.

I hope these nine expositions of "But God" texts in Scripture will help to give you a "But God" attitude. May you gain an ever-increasing appreciation for all that God has done to save sinners, and may that understanding become the chief focus of your life. May you always remember that God in his mercy and love acted to save you, just as he has for sinners throughout the ages, and just as he has spoken in his Word, all wrapped up in that two-word phrase ripe with meaning: "But God…."

ADDENDUM

If you have not come to faith in Jesus Christ and do not know the forgiveness of sins that God offers, the phrase "But God" should terrify you. It means God has been patient with you thus far in your ignorance and sin, but he will not always be so. One day he will show himself holy and just toward you, and he will punish your sins. The apostle Paul used the phrase "But God" to speak of unbelievers in his day as well. After describing a list of sins they had committed, he said their actions served "as always to fill up the measure of their sins. But God's wrath has come upon them at last!" (1 Thessalonians 2:16).

For the one who does not know Christ, "But God" means judgment and wrath, not salvation and joy. Therefore, take heed. Run to Christ. He will welcome you.

Endnotes

1. The complete account can be found in Genesis 5:28–9:29. If you haven't read it in a while, I would encourage you to do so before reading the rest of this chapter.
2. To better understand God's remembrance as grace in the Old Testament, see Exodus 2:23–25 and 1 Samuel 1:9–11.
3. Henry M. Morris, *The Genesis Record: A Scientific and Devotional Commentary on the Book of Beginnings* (Grand Rapids: Baker Book House, 1976), 177.
4. Noah's sinfulness becomes apparent at the end of his story in Scripture. After experiencing the grace of God in being delivered from the flood, Noah passes out naked in his tent, drunk from wine (Genesis 9:20–21). This story parallels the account of Adam's sin—after the "re-creation" of the world through the flood, Noah (the new Adam, as it were) tends a vineyard (like Adam working the garden) and sins (which, again like Adam, is shown through his nakedness). Thus, even after being saved from the flood, humanity cannot escape the sin problem brought about by Adam.
5. The statement in Exodus 13:18b that "the people of Israel went up out of the land of Egypt equipped for battle" does not necessarily mean they were well-armed. Instead, it "probably means organized for march rather than equipped with armor, bows, and arrows for warfare." (John D. Hannah, "Exodus," *The Bible Knowledge Commentary: Old Testament*, ed. Roy Zuck and John Walvoord [Wheaton, Ill.: Victor Books, 1985], 130).
6. Leslie Katz, "Wind May Explain Red Sea Parting," Sept 22, 2010, http://news.cnet.com/8301-17938_105-20017313-1.html (Nov 9, 2010).
7. Eugene Merrill, *Kingdom of Priests: A History of Old Testament Israel* (Grand Rapids: Baker Academic, 2008), 433.
8. I am indebted to Dr. Abner Chou of The Master's College for the analogy of planned obsolescence with regard to the old covenant.

9. For example, see Genesis 3:15; 49:8–12; Numbers 24:17; and Deuteronomy 18:15–19.

10. J.I. Packer, *Knowing God* (Downers Grove, Ill.: InterVarsity Press, 1993), 54. The chapter that contains this quote ("God Incarnate") is an excellent brief resource for understanding the incarnation.

11 . Charles Hodge, *Commentary on the Epistle to the Romans* (New York: A. C. Armstrong and Son, 1896), 214.

12 . This is known as the "Moral Influence Theory" of the atonement. Its proponents state that God can simply forgive sins because he wants to, and that he needs no sacrifice in order to do so.

13 . For an explanation and competent refutation of such teachings, see Steve Jeffery, Michael Ovey, and Andrew Sach, *Pierced for our Transgressions* (Wheaton, Ill.: Crossway Books, 2007).

14. Roger Nicole, "Postscript on Penal Substitution," in *The Glory of the Atonement: Biblical, Theological, & Practical Perspectives; Essays in Honor of Roger Nicole*, ed. Charles E. Hill III and Frank A. James (Downers Grove, Ill.: InterVarsity Press, 2004), 448.

15. From the hymn "It Is Well with My Soul" by Horatio G. Spafford, 1873.

16. John Piper, *The Passion of Jesus Christ: Fifty Reasons Why He Came to Die* (Wheaton, Ill.: Crossway Books, 2004), 11.

17. His burial is also emphasized because it fulfilled the specific prophecy of Isaiah 53:9.

18. Wayne Grudem, *Systematic Theology* (Grand Rapids: Zondervan, 2000), 1240.

19. This is far from the only place where we find this mentioned. Scripture is filled with numerous references to the doctrine of unconditional election. For a survey of many of these texts, see Steven J. Lawson, *Foundations of Grace: 1400 BC – AD 100*, A Long Line of Godly Men series (Orlando: Reformation Trust Publishing, 2006).

20. This is not to say that such people do not exist (for God does at times call even the highly esteemed members of society to himself), only that they are fairly rare.

21. To be fair, I have known many non-Calvinist believers who were gracious, humble, and kind.

22. Donald Miller, *Blue Like Jazz* (Nashville: Thomas Nelson Publishers, 2003), 238.

23. Klyne Snodgrass, Ephesians, *The NIV Application Commentary*, ed. Terry Muck (Grand Rapids: Zondervan, 1996), 100.

24. Fourth-century preacher John Chrysostom wrote: "Even faith, [Paul] says, is not from us. For if the Lord had not come, if he had not called us, how should we have been able to believe? For how, he says, shall they believe if they have not heard? So even the act of faith is not self-initiated. It is, he says, the gift of God." Cited in Mark J. Edward, ed., *Galatians, Ephesians, Philippians, Ancient Christian Commentary on Scripture*, gen. ed. Thomas C. Oden (Downers Grove, Ill.: InterVarsity Press, 1999), 134.

25. "Quickening" is used here in its older sense, meaning "life-giving"

26. "This warning clearly implies that such deception is not possible." (John MacArthur, *The MacArthur New Testament Commentary* [Nashville: Thomas Nelson Publishers, 2007], 83).

27. William D. Mounce, *Pastoral Epistles, Word Biblical Commentary*, ed. Bruce M. Metzger (Nashville: Thomas Nelson Publishers, 2000), 529.

28. For more on this subject, see John MacArthur, *The Gospel According to Jesus* (Grand Rapids: Zondervan, 1994).

ABOUT CRUCIFORM PRESS

What would a book-publishing company for gospel-centered Christians look like if it began with the realities of 21st century technology?

We think It would focus on Content, Simplicity, Reliability, Trust, Convenience, Voice, and Community. Here's what we mean by that. These are our promises to you.

Content: Every book will be helpful, inspiring, biblical, and gospel-focused.

Simplicity: Every book will be short, clear, well-written, well-edited, and accessible.

Reliability: A new book will be released the first day of each month. Every book will be the same price. Each book will have a unique cover, yet all our books will maintain a distinctive, recognizable look.

Trust: If you like this book, then you're probably a lot like us in how you think, what you believe, and how you see the world. That means you can trust us to give you only the good stuff.

Convenience: Our books will be available in print, in a variety of ebook formats, and frequently as audiobooks. Print or ebook subscription opportunities can save you time and money.

Voice: We would like to hear anything constructive you'd care to say about what we're doing and how we're doing it.

Community: We want to encourage and facilitate the sense of community that naturally exists among Christians who love the gospel of grace.

CruciformPress

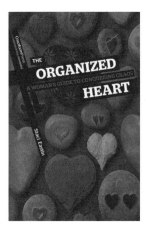

The Organized Heart
A Woman's Guide to Conquering Chaos

by Staci Eastin

**Disorganized?
You dont need more rules, the
latest technique, or a new gadget.**

*This book will show you a different,
better way. A way grounded in the
grace of God.*

"Staci Eastin packs a gracious punch, full of insights about our
disorganized hearts and lives, immediately followed by the balm of
gospel-shaped hopes. This book is ideal for accountability partners
and small groups."

> **Carolyn McCulley, blogger, filmmaker, author of *Radical
> Womanhood* and *Did I Kiss Marriage Goodbye?***

"Unless we understand the spiritual dimension of productivity, our
techniques will ultimately backfire. Find that dimension here. Encouraging and uplifting rather than guilt-driven, this book can help
women who want to be more organized but know that adding a new
method is not enough."

> **Matt Perman, Director of Strategy at Desiring God, blogger,
> author of the forthcoming book, *What's Best Next: How the
> Gospel Transforms the Way You Get Things Done***

"Organizing a home can be an insurmountable challenge for a woman. The Organized Heart makes a unique connection between idols
of the heart and the ability to run a well-managed home. This is not
a how-to. Eastin looks at sin as the root problem of disorganization.
She offers a fresh new approach and one I recommend, especially to
those of us who have tried all the other self-help models and failed."

> **Aileen Challies, Mom of three, and wife of blogger, author,
> and pastor Tim Challies**

Wrestling with an Angel
A Story of Love, Disability and the Lessons of Grace

by Greg Lucas

The riveting, inspiring true story that readers have called "a touchstone book of my life," and "alternately hilarious and heartbreaking," a book that "turns the diamond of grace in such a way that you see facets you never really noticed before."

"C.S. Lewis wrote that he paradoxically loved *The Lord of the Rings* because it 'broke his heart'—and Greg Lucas' writing does the same for me."
Justin Taylor, Managing Editor, ESV Study Bible

"Witty... stunning... striking... humorous and heartfelt. *Wrestling with an Angel* provides a fresh, honest look at one father's struggle to embrace God in the midst of his son's disability. Can sheer laughter and weeping gracefully coexist in a world of so much affliction? Greg knows all about it. I highly recommend this wonderfully personal book!"
Joni Eareckson Tada, Joni and Friends International

"You will laugh; you will cry. You will feel sick; you will feel inspired. You will be repulsed by the ugliness of sin; you will be overwhelmed by the love of God. Greg Lucas takes us on an unforgettable ride as he extracts the most beautiful insights into grace from the most painful experiences of life."
David P. Murray, Puritan Reformed Theological Seminary

"Greg Lucas is a captivating storyteller. When he writes about life with Jake, I recognize God's grace and loving persistence in my life. I want more!"
Noël Piper, author, and wife of pastor and author John Piper

Download our Free 109-page sampler

CruciformPress

Yours to

Download,
Share, Print,
Read,

Whatever

CRUCIFORM
SAMPLER

EXCERPTS FROM OUR FIRST SIX BOOKS:

Tim Challies **Sexual Detox**

Greg Lucas **Wrestling with an Angel**

Nate Palmer **Servanthood as Worship**

Dan Cruver, Editor **Reclaiming Adoption**

Tad Thompson **Intentional Parenting**

Staci Eastin **The Organized Heart**

Download it at http://bit.ly/samplr